ASHOKAN FAREWELL

by
JAY UNGAR

arranged for harp by
DEBORAH FRIOU

from the soundtrack of the PBS Series
"THE CIVIL WAR"

Ashokan Farewell

Arranged for harp by Deborah Friou

Music by Jay Ungar

Folk harpers set C below middle C to C natural. The C above middle C will change.

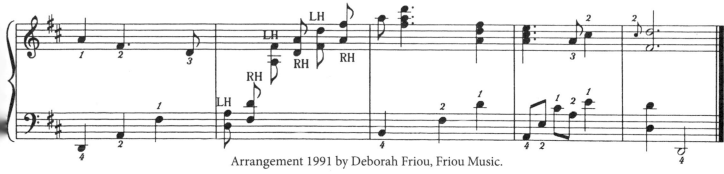

Arrangement 1991 by Deborah Friou, Friou Music.
P.O. Box 157, Brunswick, ME 04011

Harp Music by Deborah Friou

Harp Books

Renaissance Music for the Harp

Early Music for the Harp

Harp Exercises for Agility and Speed

Rodgers and Hammerstein for the Harp

Ballads and Court Dances

Baroque Music for the Harp

Yuletide Treasure

Classical Music for the Harp

Sheet Music for the Harp

Danny Boy

Scarborough Fair

Ashokan Farewell

To Drive the Cold Winter Away

Kum Ba Yah

Be Thou My Vision

Auld Lang Syne

Dona Nobis Pacem

Recordings

Renaissance Muse

Harper's Dream

Yuletide Treasure

Cover Art by Steve Duglas

DISTRIBUTED BY HAL LEONARD

0 73999 88818 8

00722590   U.S. $7.95

ISBN-13: 978-0-9628120-1-9

50795

9 780962 812019